Jonathan Edwards' Resolutions
And Advice to Young Converts

Introduced and edited
by Stephen J. Nichols

PUBLISHING
P.O. BOX 817 • PHILLIPSBURG • NEW JERSEY 08865-0817

© 2001 by Stephen J. Nichols

Illustration on the cover and page 7: "Artist's Conception of Main Street, Northampton, 1786" by Maitland de Gorgorza. Commissioned in 1936 for the 150th anniversary of the *Daily Hampshire Gazette*. Used by permission of Forbes Library, Northampton, Massachusetts.

Illustration on page 21: "The Edwards Memorial" by Herbert Adams. A life-size bronze plaque located at First Church, Northampton, Massachusetts. This plaque was unveiled on June 22, 1900, 150 years after Edwards'dismissal from his Northampton pulpit. Reproduced from a photograph in the Forbes Library, Northampton, Massachusetts.

Library of Congress Cataloging-in-Publication Data

Edwards, Jonathan, 1703–1758.
    [Resolutions]
    Jonathan Edwards' Resolutions ; and, Advice to young converts / introduced and edited by Stephen J. Nichols.
    p. cm.
    ISBN-10: 0-87552-189-4 (pbk.)
    ISBN-13: 978-0-87552-189-3 (pbk.)
    1. Christian life—Early works to 1800. 2. Young adults—Religious life—Early works to 1800. I. Nichols, Stephen J., 1970– II. Edwards, Jonathan, 1703–1758. Advice to young converts. III. Title.

BV4501.3 E399 2001
248'.4'858—dc21

                                        2001032892

CONTENTS

List of Illustrations   4
Introduction   5
Resolutions   17
Advice to Young Converts   27
For Further Reading   37

LIST OF ILLUSTRATIONS

1. Main Street, Northampton, in 1786　　　7
2. Jonathan Edwards Memorial　　　21
3. Cover of 1821 edition of *Advice to Young Converts*　　　31

INTRODUCTION

This booklet brings together two unique and remarkable texts by the colonial divine Jonathan Edwards. The first is his *Resolutions,* written during the years 1722 and 1723. When he wrote these seventy resolutions, Edwards was completing his schooling and ministerial training and was anticipating setting out on his life's work. He took advantage of the opportunity to pause and reflect on the type of person he wanted to be and the way in which he wanted to live his life.

In a manner that would come to typify his entire career, he took up his pen and, in the moments of quiet he could wrest from a busy day, wrote the guidelines, the system of checks and balances he would use to chart out his life—his relationships, his conversations, his desires, his activities. In short, through these resolutions he offers himself his own advice.

The second text, *Advice to Young Converts,* is not all that different from the *Resolutions.* It too consists of advice to a young person, only this advice comes in the form of a letter. And Edwards, a few years wiser, is now being called upon to guide others. Though not as broad in scope as the *Resolutions,* this letter reveals a wealth of information and insight into successfully living the Christian life. The letter was written during a fascinating period of colonial times and of Edwards' life, the time known as the Great Awakening, spanning the years 1740–1742. In the letter he offers young Deborah Hatheway nineteen separate points to consider. The letter presents not just timely advice for her, but timeless advice for generations to come. As one scholar recently observed, the letter "has become a classic of Christian devotion."

Neither one of the original manuscripts of these texts has survived. Both texts, however, have been widely reproduced and printed throughout the last three centuries. The American Tract Society distributed hundreds of thousands of copies of *Advice to Young Converts* throughout the nineteenth century, and the *Resolutions* has been reprinted since the 1700s. Both texts are reproduced again here, with extremely minor revisions that update the grammar, for a new generation of young converts in the hope that these words of Edwards will continue to be used by God in encouraging us along in our "Christian course."

Today's bookstores are overrun by "how to" books. Edwards' advice to Deborah Hatheway and to himself, however, stands in a class by itself. His straightforward and biblically sound advice helps cut through the static and returns our focus to Christ and to his revelation as that which alone guides our steps.

Life of Jonathan Edwards

Born on October 5, 1703, Jonathan Edwards grew up in a minister's home in East Windsor, Connecticut. At the age of 13, he entered Yale, receiving his B.A. degree in 1720 and his M.A. in 1723. For a brief pe-

Artist's Conception of Main Street, Northampton, Massachusetts, 1786. Drawn by Maitland de Gorgorza.

riod in 1722–1723 he pastored a Presbyterian church in New York City, and then he returned to Yale as a tutor or instructor for a few years. In 1727 he answered the call to serve as an assistant minister at Northampton Congregational Church in Massachusetts.

Following the death of Solomon Stoddard, Edwards assumed the role of minister at Northampton in 1729, a position he held until 1750. During this time he was a catalyst for both a series of revivals in the mid-1730s and also the Great Awakening in 1740–1742. He also published a number of sermons and treatises, including *A Treatise Concerning Religious Affections* in 1746. Through his preaching and writing Edwards quickly gained an international reputation as perhaps the colonies' foremost pastor, theologian, and intellectual.

Ironically Edwards was dismissed from the Northampton pulpit in 1750. He then moved to the frontier town of Stockbridge, Massachusetts, where he served as minister at the missionary outpost to the Native American Mohawk and Mohican tribes. He continued to write, publishing such works as *Freedom of the Will* (1754) and *Original Sin* (1758).

Trustees of the College of New Jersey, now Princeton University, prevailed on Edwards to serve as president. In January 1758 Edwards assumed the role. Only a few months later, however, he suffered an adverse reaction to a smallpox inoculation and died on March 22.

Edwards left behind quite a legacy through his eleven children and seventy-two grandchildren, as well as his numerous writings, many of which were published after his death. Through these writings Edwards continues his lifelong occupation of ministering to the church.

Resolutions

Edwards spent the majority of his life in the Connecticut River Valley. From the time of his birth in 1703 until 1750, he lived up and down the Connecticut River in both Connecticut and Massachusetts, except, that is, for a few months in 1722 and 1723. Young Jonathan left his home and familiar surroundings to answer a call to minister to a small Presbyterian congregation in New York City. His new pastoral charge located him somewhere in the vicinity of modern day Broad and Wall streets.

He was no stranger to adventure. As a student at Yale, he moved a few times along with his institution, primarily due to the fact that Yale had not yet found a permanent home, but also due in part to an attempt to avoid skirmishes with the forces that would eventually engage in the Seven Years' War. But now nineteen-year-old Edwards found himself in a new environment, in a new situation, and with a new and rather weighty responsibility.

To face these new challenges, Edwards, following the pattern he established early on and continued to hone throughout his life, took to writing. Like many of his Puritan forebears, he started a diary as a window into his own soul and innermost thoughts, as a way to gauge his relationship to Christ and monitor his spiritual condition. He also started a series of guidelines not only to measure his life, but also to set goals for himself. In essence they came to serve as a personal mission statement.

Edwards begins his *Resolutions* with a solemn reminder: "I am unable to do anything without God's help." He excelled in his studies at Yale, graduating at the top of his class for his B.A. and continuing to stand head and shoulders above his classmates in his master's program. Gifted, capable, and well-trained, Edwards, however, realizes his absolute dependence on God, and this becomes the key ingredient to the *Resolutions*. Far from an advocate for self-help, Edwards realizes that anything he might do that pleases God or anything that amounts to something of significance is only the result of God working through him. Nevertheless, Edwards also acknowledges his need for self-discipline.

As you read the *Resolutions*, you cannot help but see Edwards' resolve to bring all areas of his life under control. This challenge permeates the entire text. No aspect of life goes unnoticed. He addresses everything from eating and drinking to conversations, from prayer and Bible reading to relationships with his family, from his spiritual life to his deepest desires—no stone remains unturned. Following James' teaching, Edwards even pays attention to the disproportionately small in size but significant and dominant member of the body, the tongue. Edwards realizes what great harm the tongue can produce and what great trouble it can get him into, and he directs many of his resolutions to taming this unruly member.

The *Resolutions* also reveal Edwards' utmost determination to bring every area of his life under subjection of the Lordship of Christ and to rest in the sovereignty of God. The ancient Greeks spoke of the *summum bonum,* or the highest good. By this they meant that, while there are indeed many good things for which one can live, something stands out as the best, or the highest, of those good things. For Edwards, broadly speaking, the first question of the *Westminster Catechism* captures the answer perfectly. The highest good that anyone can do—or to use the catechism's language, our chief end—is "to glorify God and enjoy him forever." Many of Edwards' resolutions represent his attempt to make this broad statement concrete and specific in his own life. He is concerned that Christ has preeminence and the Bible has priority in all that he does. He wants his life—indeed his days, weeks, and months—not to be squandered on even the things that are good. Instead, he wants the best and commits himself to it.

Edwards begins dating the resolutions on December 18, 1722, with entry number 35, the same day he begins his diary. He concludes the resolutions on August 17, 1723. While the earlier resolutions are not dated, they probably were written shortly before he began dating them. He went to New York in August of 1722 and remained there until April 1723. From then until the fall of 1723, Edwards remained at his family's home in East Windsor, writing his master's thesis and providing pulpit supply for various churches. Consequently the *Resolutions* came at a transitional time in Edwards' life. He was moving from his foundational and formative years as a student to the period in which he began his profession as a churchman and theologian. Throughout his life the *Resolutions* were his constant companion.

Edwards prefaces his *Resolutions* with an exhortation to "remember to read over these resolutions once a week." Perhaps this bit of advice is also worthy of imitation. The *Resolutions* are as relevant today as they were when he first penned them so long ago. Reading through them on a regular basis may very well help us also to live with all of our might to the glory and praise of God.

Advice to Young Converts

After receiving his master's degree, Edwards served for a few years as a tutor or instructor at Yale until 1727, when he moved to Northampton. He would spend the majority of his ministry years at Northampton until 1750. During Edwards' stay at Northampton, he went through many hills and valleys with his congregation. One highlight, of course, is the time during which Edwards writes this letter, the time known as the Great Awakening.

Next to the Revolutionary War, the Great Awakening is perhaps the most remarkable event in the Colonial period, and it certainly marks the busiest time in Edwards' life. Despite the increasing demands on him, Edwards nevertheless took the time to write a rather long letter to a young Christian woman in the nearby town of Suffield, Connecticut. The congregation in Suffield was currently without a pastor for a short time. The church did have some rather fascinating visitors, however. George Whitefield preached in Suffield during one of his tours through the New England colonies in 1740. And in the spring months of

1741, Jonathan Edwards also visited and ministered to the congregation. A few months later, when Deborah Hatheway, a young member of the congregation, needed spiritual guidance, she looked to the minister from Northampton.

Edwards, well known for his ability as a preacher, as evidenced in such sermons as *Sinners in the Hands of an Angry God*, and as an author, as evidenced in such books as *A Treatise Concerning Religious Affections*, *History of the Work of Redemption*, and *Freedom of the Will*, displays here another dimension of his life: his intense concern for the spiritual life of others and his ability to gently and gracefully shepherd a young Christian. Here we see Edwards as pastor, deeply caring for those who look to him for guidance and help. When he received Miss Hatheway's request, he viewed his response as no less important or crucial a task than drafting his sermons, writing his books, or corresponding with his Bostonian and Scottish ministerial colleagues. By many accounts Edwards remains America's foremost theologian, and here we see him patiently guiding a young Christian through some basics of the Christian life.

After a short introduction Edwards offers nineteen separate points of advice. A few overarching themes emerge from this letter. First, Edwards emphasizes an awareness of and sensitivity to sin. "Though God has forgiven and forgotten your past sins," he writes, "yet don't forget them yourself." His goal is not to leave Deborah, or us for that matter, wallowing in our sins and in a state of depression over our past. In fact he warns against this by urging Deborah not to "consume too much of [her] time and strength in poring and puzzling over past experiences." Rather he wants her and us to be humble, to never forget the magnitude of God's grace in redeeming us from our sins.

Such a sense of our sin further serves to remind us of our constant need to be on guard against the subtle ways sin can creep into our lives and take root in our hearts, especially after our conversion. So Edwards, echoing Paul's injunction in Philippians 3:12–14, reminds us to strive earnestly after Christ's work in our lives. Perhaps one of the letter's most poignant moments comes in Edwards' eighteenth point, where he observes that Christ takes us as helpless children, cleanses us through his blood, and covers us in his righteousness.

The sense of sin should also lead to a deep gratitude to God that demonstrates itself in service to him. Edwards does not shrink from reminding Deborah Hatheway of her "duty" and encourages her to take seriously her responsibilities to pray, take the sacraments, worship God, and minister to and care for others. Edwards also reminds her that she has a responsibility to live her life so as to reflect Christ living in her. "Don't let the adversaries of religion have any grounds," he solemnly expresses, "to say that these converts don't carry themselves any better than others."

A final theme that emerges in the letter concerns the primacy of the church and Deborah's involvement in it. She is not isolated, on her own, or independent. Rather she belongs to the body of Christ, and throughout the letter Edwards reminds her that she lives within the community of Christ and as a member of his body. Edwards ends the letter by drawing her attention to the work of God beyond the church at Suffield, and models his own dependence on the body of Christ by humbly asking for her prayers on his behalf.

In addition to these larger themes, Edwards offers many proverbial pieces of advice, such as "When you hear sermons hear them for yourself." He also offers very practical points, such as his caution when she counsels her peers. He wisely directs her to counsel, not from a posture of superiority, but with an acknowledgment of her own unworthiness. The letter overflows with such sage advice that speaks to us just as meaningfully as it spoke to Deborah Hatheway.

Through these two texts, which he probably never intended for such a public audience, Edwards continues to minister to the church. These texts, however, present a side of Edwards that is little known. Just one month after he wrote this letter to Deborah Hatheway, Edwards preached his famous sermon, *Sinners in the Hands of an Angry God*. The most read of all of his writings, this sermon is the only writing of Edwards that most people will ever read. On the one hand, there is nothing wrong with this: *Sinners* is a great sermon, worthy of its popularity. On the other hand, it is somewhat unfortunate that most will know only the Edwards of *Sinners*. These texts demonstrate that there is much more to the thought and writings of this colonial divine. And arguably they attest to the fact that, for those willing to listen, Jonathan Edwards still has much to offer the church today.

RESOLUTIONS

Being sensible that I am unable to do anything without God's help, I do humbly entreat him by his grace to enable me to keep these resolutions, so far as they are agreeable to his will, for Christ's sake.

Remember to read over these resolutions once a week.

1. Resolved, that I will do whatsoever I think to be most to God's glory and to my own good, profit, and pleasure, in the whole of my duration, without any consideration of the time, whether now or never so many myriads of ages hence. Resolved to do whatever I think to be my duty, and most for the good and advantage of mankind in general. Resolved to do this, whatever difficulties I meet with, how ever so many and how ever so great.

2. Resolved, to be continually endeavoring to find out some new invention and contrivance to promote the forementioned things.

3. Resolved, if ever I shall fall and grow dull, so as to neglect to keep any part of these resolutions, to repent of all I can remember, when I come to myself again.

4. Resolved, never to do any manner of thing, whether in soul or body, less or more, but what tends to the glory of God; nor be, nor suffer it, if I can possibly avoid it.

5. Resolved, never to lose one moment of time; but improve it the most profitable way I possibly can.

6. Resolved, to live with all my might, while I do live.

7. Resolved, never to do anything that I should be afraid to do if it were the last hour of my life.

8. Resolved, to act, in all respects, both speaking and doing, as if nobody had been so vile as I, and as if I had committed the same sins, or had the same infirmities or failings as others; and to let the knowledge of their failings promote nothing but shame in myself, and prove only an occasion of my confessing my own sins and misery to God.

9. Resolved, to think much on all occasions of my own dying, and of the common circumstances which attend death.

10. Resolved, when I feel pain, to think of the pains of martyrdom and of hell.

11. Resolved, when I think of any theorem in divinity to be solved, immediately to do what I can toward solving it, if circumstances don't hinder.

12. Resolved, if I take delight in it as a gratification of pride or vanity or on any such account, immediately to throw it by.

13. Resolved, to be endeavoring to find out fit objects of charity and liberality.

14. Resolved, never to do anything out of revenge.

15. Resolved, never to suffer the least motions of anger to irrational beings.

16. Resolved, never to speak evil of anyone, so that it shall tend to his dishonor, more or less, upon no account except for some real good.

17. Resolved, that I will live so as I shall wish I had done when I come to die.

18. Resolved, to live so at all times as I think is best in my devout frames, and when I have clearest notions of things of the gospel and another world.

19. Resolved, never to do anything that I should be afraid to do if I expected it would not be above an hour before I should hear the last trump.

20. Resolved, to maintain the strictest temperance in eating and drinking.

21. Resolved, never to do anything that, if I should see it in another, I should count a just occasion to despise him for, or think any way the more meanly of him.

22. Resolved, to endeavor to obtain for myself as much happiness in the other world as I possibly can, with all the power, might, vigor, and vehemence, yea violence, I am capable of, or can bring myself to exert, in any way that can be thought of.

23. Resolved, frequently to take some deliberate action that seems most unlikely to be done, for the glory of God, and trace it back to the original intention, designs, and ends of it; and if I find it not to be for God's glory, to repute it as a breach of the 4th resolution.

24. Resolved, whenever I do any conspicuously evil action, to trace it back till I come to the original cause; and then both carefully endeavor to do so no more, and to fight and pray with all my might against the original of it.

25. Resolved, to examine carefully and constantly what that one thing in me is that causes me in the least to doubt the love of God; and so direct all my forces against it.

26. Resolved, to cast away such things as I find do abate my assurance.

27. Resolved, never willfully to omit anything unless the omission is for the glory of God; and frequently to examine my omissions.

28. Resolved, to study the Scriptures so steadily, constantly, and frequently that I may find, and plainly perceive myself to grow in the knowledge of them.

29. Resolved, never to count that a prayer, nor to let that pass as a prayer or as a petition of a prayer, which is so made that I cannot hope that God will answer it; nor that as a confession, which I cannot hope God will accept.

30. Resolved, to strive to my utmost every week to be brought higher in religion, and to a higher exercise of grace, than I was the week before.

31. Resolved, never to say anything at all against anybody, but when it is perfectly agreeable to the highest degree of Christian honor and of love to mankind, agreeable to the lowest humility and a sense of my own faults and failings, and agreeable to the Golden Rule; often, when I have said anything against anyone, to bring it to, and try it strictly by, the test of this resolution.

32. Resolved, to be strictly and firmly faithful to my trust, that that in Proverbs 20:6, "A faithful man who can find?" may not be partly fulfilled in me.

33. Resolved, always to do what I can towards making, maintaining, and preserving peace, when it can be without over-balancing detriment in other respects. (Dec. 26, 1722)

34. Resolved, in narrations never to speak anything but the pure and simple verity.

35. Resolved, whenever I so much question whether I have done my duty that my quiet and calm is thereby disturbed, to set it down, and also how the question was resolved. (Dec. 18, 1722)

36. Resolved, never to speak evil of any, except I have some particular good call for it. (Dec. 19, 1722)

The Edwards Memorial. A life-size bronze plaque mounted at First Church, Northampton. Sculpted by Herbert Adams.

37. Resolved, to inquire every night, as I am going to bed, wherein I have been negligent, what sin I have committed, and wherein I have denied myself; also to inquire so at the end of every week, month, and year. (Dec. 22 & 26, 1722)

38. Resolved, never to speak anything that is sportive or a matter of laughter on the Lord's day. (Sabbath evening, Dec. 23, 1722)

39. Resolved, never to do anything that I so much question the lawfulness of, as that I intend, at the same time, to consider and examine afterwards whether it be lawful or not: unless I as much question the lawfulness of the omission.

40. Resolved, to inquire every night, before I go to bed, whether I have acted in the best way I possibly could, with respect to eating and drinking. (Jan. 7, 1723)

41. Resolved, to ask myself at the end of every day, week, month, and year, wherein I could possibly in any respect have done better. (Jan. 11, 1723)

42. Resolved, frequently to renew the dedication of myself to God, which was made at my baptism; which I solemnly renewed when I was received into the communion of the church; and which I have solemnly remade this 12th day of January, 1723.

43. Resolved, never henceforward till I die, to act as if I were any way my own, but to act entirely and altogether as God's, agreeable to what is to be found in Saturday, Jan. 12.

44. Resolved, that no other end but religion shall have any influence at all on any of my actions; and that no action shall be, in the least circumstance, any otherwise than the religious end will carry it. (Jan. 12, 1723)

45. Resolved, never to allow any pleasure or grief, joy or sorrow, nor any affection at all, nor any degree of affection, nor any circumstance relating to it, but what helps religion. (Jan. 12 & 13, 1723)

46. Resolved, never to allow the least measure of any fretting uneasiness at my father or mother. Resolved to suffer no effects of it, so much as in the least alteration of speech, or motion of my eye: and to be especially careful of it with respect to any of our family.

47. Resolved, to endeavor to my utmost to deny whatever is not most agreeable to a temper that is good, and universally sweet and benevolent, quiet, peaceable, contented and easy, compassionate and generous, humble and meek, submissive and obliging, diligent and industrious, charitable and even, patient, moderate, forgiving, and sincere; and to do at all times what such a temper would lead me to. Examine strictly every week, whether I have done so. (Sabbath morning, May 5, 1723)

48. Resolved, constantly, with the utmost niceness and diligence and with the strictest scrutiny, to be looking into the state of my soul, that I may know whether I have truly an interest in Christ or not; that when I come to die, I may not have any negligence respecting this to repent of. (May 26, 1723)

49. Resolved, that this never shall be, if I can help it.

50. Resolved, I will act so as I think I shall judge would have been best and most prudent when I come into the future world. (July 5, 1723)

51. Resolved, that I will act so, in every respect, as I think I shall wish I had done if I should at last be damned. (July 8, 1723)

52. I frequently hear persons in old age say how they would live if they were to live their lives over

again. Resolved, that I will live just so as I can think I shall wish I had done, supposing I live to old age. (July 8, 1723)

53. Resolved, to improve every opportunity, when I am in the best and happiest frame of mind, to cast and venture my soul on the Lord Jesus Christ, to trust and confide in him, and consecrate myself wholly to him; that from this I may have assurance of my safety, knowing that I confide in my Redeemer. (July 8, 1723)

54. Whenever I hear anything spoken in commendation of any person, if I think it would be praiseworthy in me, resolved to endeavor to imitate it. (July 8, 1723)

55. Resolved, to endeavor to my utmost to act as I can think I should do if I had already seen the happiness of heaven and the torments of hell. (July 8, 1723)

56. Resolved, never to give over, nor in the least to slacken my fight with my corruptions, however unsuccessful I may be.

57. Resolved, when I fear misfortunes and adversities, to examine whether I have done my duty, and resolve to do it; and let it be just as Providence orders it. I will, as far as I can, be concerned about nothing but my duty and my sin. (June 9 & July 13, 1723)

58. Resolved, not only to refrain from an air of dislike, fretfulness, and anger in conversation, but to exhibit an air of love, cheerfulness, and benignity. (May 27 & July 13, 1723)

59. Resolved, when I am most conscious of provocations to ill-nature and anger, that I will strive most to feel and act good-naturedly; yea, at such times, to manifest good nature, though I think that in other respects it would be disadvantageous, and so as would be imprudent at other times. (May 12, July 11, & July 13)

60. Resolved, whenever my feelings begin to appear in the least out of order, when I am conscious of the least uneasiness within, or the least irregularity without, I will then subject myself to the strictest examination. (July 4 & 13, 1723)

61. Resolved, that I will not give way to that listlessness which I find unbends and relaxes my mind from being fully and fixedly set on religion, whatever excuse I may have for it—that what my listlessness inclines me to do is best to be done, etc. (May 21 & July 13, 1723)

62. Resolved, never to do anything but duty; and then according to Ephesians 6:6–8, do it willingly and cheerfully "as unto the Lord, and not to man; knowing that whatever good thing any man does, the same shall he receive of the Lord." (June 25 & July 13, 1723)

63. On the supposition, that there never was to be but one individual in the world at any one time who was properly a complete Christian, in all respects of a right stamp, having Christianity always shining in its true luster, and appearing excellent and lovely from whatever part and under whatever character viewed: Resolved, to act just as I would if I strove with all my might to be that one who should live in my time. (Jan. 14 & July 13, 1723)

64. Resolved, when I find those "groanings which cannot be uttered" of which the Apostle speaks and those "breakings of soul for the longing it has" of which the Psalmist speaks, Psalm 119:20, that I will promote them to the utmost of my power, and that I will not be weary of earnestly endeavoring to vent my desires, nor of the repetitions of such earnestness. (July 23 & Aug. 10, 1723)

65. Resolved, very much to exercise myself in this all my life long, that is, with the greatest openness I am capable of, to declare my ways to God, and lay open my soul to him: all my sins, temptations, difficulties, sorrows, fears, hopes, desires, and everything, and every circumstance; according to Dr. Manton's sermon on Psalm 119:26 (July 26 & Aug 10, 1723) [Thomas Manton, *One Hundred and Ninety Sermons on the Hundred and Nineteenth Psalm* (London, 1861).]

66. Resolved, that I will endeavor always to keep a benign aspect, and air of acting and speaking in all places and in all companies, except it should so happen that duty requires otherwise.

67. Resolved, after afflictions to inquire what I am the better for them, what good I have got by them, and what I might have got by them.

68. Resolved, to confess frankly to myself all that which I find in myself, either infirmity or sin; and, if it be what concerns religion, also to confess the whole case to God and to implore needed help. (July 23 & Aug. 10, 1723)

69. Resolved, always to do that which I shall wish I had done when I see others do it. (Aug. 11, 1723)

70. Let there be something of benevolence in all that I speak. (Aug. 17, 1723)

ADVICE TO YOUNG CONVERTS

Dear Child,

As you desired me to send you in writing some directions on how to conduct yourself in your Christian course, I will now answer your request. The sweet remembrance of the great things I have lately seen at Suffield, and the dear affections for those persons I have conversed with there, give good evidences of a saving work of God upon their hearts and also incline me to do anything that lies in my power to contribute to the spiritual joy and prosperity of God's people there. And what I write to you, I would also say to other young women there who are your friends and companions and the children of God. Therefore, I desire you would communicate it to them as you have opportunity.

1. I would advise you to keep up as great a strife and earnestness in religion in all aspects of it, as you would do if you knew yourself to be in a state of nature and you were seeking conversion. We advise persons under convictions to be extremely earnest for the kingdom of heaven, but when they have attained conversion they ought not to be the less watchful, laborious, and earnest in the whole work of religion, but the more; for they are under infinitely greater obligations. For lack of this, many persons in a few months after their conversion have begun to lose the sweet and lively sense of spiritual things, and to grow cold and

flat and dark. They have pierced themselves through with many sorrows, whereas if they had done as the Apostle did in Philippians 3:12–14, their path would have been as the shining light, which shines more and more unto the perfect day.

> Not that I have already all this, or have already been made perfect, but I press on to take hold of that which Christ Jesus took hold of me. Brothers, I do not consider myself yet to have taken hold of it. But one thing I do: Forgetting what is behind and straining toward what is ahead, I press on toward the goal to win the prize for which God has called me heavenward in Christ Jesus. (Phil. 3:12–14)

2. Don't slack off seeking, striving, and praying for the very same things that we exhort unconverted persons to strive for, and a degree of which you have had in conversion. Thus pray that your eyes may be opened, that you may receive your sight, that you may know your self and be brought to God's feet, and that you may see the glory of God and Christ, may be raised from the dead, and have the love of Christ shed abroad in your heart. Those that have most of these things still need to pray for them; for there is so much blindness and hardness and pride and death remaining that they still need to have that work of God upon them, further to enlighten and enliven them. This will be a further bringing out of darkness into God's marvelous light, and a kind of new conversion and resurrection from the dead. There are very few requests that are not only proper for a natu-

ral person, but that in some sense are also proper for the godly.

3. When you hear sermons, hear them for yourself, even though what is spoken in them may be more especially directed to the unconverted or to those that in other respects are in different circumstances from yourself. Let the chief intent of your mind be to consider what ways you can apply the things that you are hearing in the sermon. You should ask, What improvement should I make, based on these things, for my own soul's good?

4. Though God has forgiven and forgotten your past sins, yet don't forget them yourself. Often remember what a wretched bond slave you were in the land of Egypt. Often bring to mind your particular acts of sin before conversion, as the blessed Apostle Paul is often mentioning his old blaspheming, persecuting, and injuriousness, to the renewed humbling of his heart and acknowledging that he was the least of the apostles, and not worthy to be called an apostle, and the least of saints, and the chief of sinners. And be often in confessing your old sins to God. Also, let this following passage be often in your mind: "Then, when I make atonement for all you have done, you will remember and be ashamed and never again open your mouth because of your humiliation, declares the sovereign LORD" (Ezek. 16:63).

5. Remember that you have more cause, on some accounts a thousand times more, to lament and humble yourself for sins that have been since conversion than those that were before conversion, because of the infinitely greater obligations that are upon you to live to God. Look upon the faithfulness of Christ in un-

changeably continuing his loving favor, and the unspeakable and saving fruits of his everlasting love. Despite all your great unworthiness since your conversion, his grace remains as great or as wonderful as it was in converting you.

6. Be always greatly humbled by your remaining sin, and never think that you lie low enough for it, but yet don't be at all discouraged or disheartened by it. Although we are exceeding sinful, we have an advocate with the Father, Jesus Christ the righteous, the preciousness of whose blood, the merit of whose righteousness, and the greatness of whose love and faithfulness infinitely overtop the highest mountains of our sins.

7. When you engage in the duty of prayer, come to the sacrament of the Lord's Supper, or attend any other duty of divine worship, come to Christ as Mary Magdalene did.

> When a woman who had lived a sinful life in that town learned that Jesus was eating at the Pharisee's house, she brought an alabaster jar of perfume, and as she stood behind him at his feet weeping, she began to wet his feet with her tears. Then she wiped them with her hair, kissed them and poured perfume on them. (Luke 7:37–38)

Just like her, come and cast yourself down at his feet and kiss them, and pour forth upon him the sweet perfumed ointment of divine love, out of a pure and broken heart, as she poured her precious ointment out of her pure, alabaster, broken box.

ADVICE TO YOUNG CONVERTS.

PUBLISHED FOR THE

HARTFORD EVANGELICAL TRACT SOCIETY.

AND TO BE HAD OF THEIR AGENT, BARZILLAI
HUDSON, JUN. IN HARTFORD, AND AT
THEIR DEPOSITORIES IN THE PRIN-
CIPAL TOWNS IN THIS STATE.

Price, 1 cent; or $1 per 100.

HARTFORD, CONN.
1821.

Cover of the Hartford Evangelical Tract Society's
1821 edition of *Advice to Young Converts*.

8. Remember that pride is the worst viper that is in the heart, the greatest disturber of the soul's peace and sweet communion with Christ. It was the first sin that ever was, and lies lowest in the foundation of Satan's whole building. It is the most difficult to root out, and it is the most hidden, secret, and deceitful of all lust, and it often creeps in, insensibly, into the midst of religion and sometimes under the disguise of humility.

9. That you may pass a good judgment on your spiritual condition, always consider your best conversations and best experiences to be the ones that produce the following two effects: first, those conversations and experiences that make you least, lowest, and most like a little child; and, second, those that do most engage and fix your heart in a full and firm disposition to deny yourself for God and to spend and be spent for him.

10. If at any time you fall into doubts about the state of your soul under darkness and dull frames of mind, it is proper to look over past experiences. Don't, however, consume too much of your time and strength in poring and puzzling thoughts about old experiences, that in dull frames appear dim and are very much out of sight, at least as to that which is the cream and life and sweetness of them. Rather, apply yourself with all your might to an earnest pursuit after renewed experiences, new light, and new, lively acts of faith and love. One new discovery of the glory of Christ's face, and the fountain of his sweet grace and love will do more towards scattering clouds of darkness and doubting in one minute than examining old experiences by the best mark that can be given for a whole year.

11. When the exercise of grace is at a low ebb, and

corruption prevails, and by that means fear prevails, don't desire to have fear cast out any other way than by the reviving and prevailing of love, for it is not agreeable to the method of God's wise dispensations that it should be cast out any other way. When love is asleep, the saints need fear to restrain them from sin, and therefore it is so ordered that at such times fear comes upon them, and that more or less as love sinks. But when love is in lively exercise, persons don't need fear. The prevailing of love in the heart naturally tends to cast out fear as darkness in a room vanishes away as you let more and more of the perfect beams of the sun into it: "There is no fear in love. But perfect love drives out fear, because fear has to do with punishment. The one who fears is not made perfect in love." (1 John 4:18)

12. You should be often exhorting and counseling and warning others, especially at such a day as this: "Let us not give up meeting together, as some are in the habit of doing, but let us encourage one another—and all the more as you see the Day approaching" (Heb. 10:25).

And I would advise you especially to be much in exhorting children and young women who are your equals; and when you exhort others that are men, I would advise that you take opportunities for it chiefly when you are alone with them or when only young persons are present.

> I also want women to dress modestly, with de-
> cency and propriety, not with braided hair or
> gold or pearls or expensive clothes, but with
> good deeds, appropriate for women who profess

to worship God. A woman should learn in quietness and full submission. (1 Tim. 2:9–11)

13. When you counsel and warn others, do it earnestly, affectionately, and thoroughly. And when you are speaking to your equals, let your warnings be intermixed with expressions of your sense of your own unworthiness and of the sovereign grace that makes you differ. And, if you can with a good conscience, say how you in yourself are more unworthy than they.

14. If you would set up religious meetings of young women by yourselves, to be attended once in a while, besides the other meetings that you attend, I should think it would be very proper and profitable.

15. Under special difficulties, or when in great need of or great longings after any particular mercies for your self or others, set apart a day of secret fasting and prayer alone. Let the day be spent not only in petitions for the mercies you desired, but in searching your heart, and looking over your past life, and confessing your sins before God, not as practiced in public prayer, but by a very particular rehearsal before God. Include the sins of your past life from your childhood up until now, both before and after conversion, with particular circumstances and aggravations. Also be very particular and as thorough as possible, spreading all the abominations of your heart before him.

16. Don't let the adversaries of religion have any grounds to say that these converts don't carry themselves any better than others.

If you love those who love you, what reward will you get? Are not even the tax collectors

doing that? And if you greet only your broth-
ers, what are you doing more than others? Do
not even pagans do that? Be perfect, therefore,
as your heavenly Father is perfect. (Matt.
5:46–48)

How holy should the children of God be! And the
redeemed and the ones beloved of the Son of God
should behave themselves in a manner worthy of
Christ. Therefore walk as a child of the light and of
the day, and adorn the doctrine of God your Savior.
Particularly be much in those things that may especially be called Christian virtues, that make you like
the Lamb of God. Be meek and lowly of heart and full
of a pure, heavenly, and humble love to all. Abound in
deeds of love to others and of self-denial for others,
and let there be in you a disposition to account others
better than yourself.

17. Don't talk of things of religion and matters of
experience with an air of lightness and laughter, which
is too much the custom in many places.

18. In all your course, walk with God and follow
Christ as a little, poor, helpless child, taking hold of
Christ's hand, keeping your eye on the mark of the
wounds on his hands and side. From these wounds
came the blood that cleanses you from sin and hides
your nakedness under the skirt of the white shining
robe of his righteousness.

19. Pray much for the church of God and especially that he would carry on his glorious work that he
has now begun. Be much in prayer for the ministers of
Christ.

Particularly I would beg a special interest in your

prayers and the prayers of your Christian companions, both when you are alone and when you are together, for your affectionate friend, that rejoices over you and desires to be your servant.

In Jesus Christ,
JONATHAN EDWARDS

For Further Reading

Edwards, Jonathan. *A Jonathan Edwards Reader*. Edited by John E. Smith, Harry S. Stout, and Kenneth P. Minkema. New Haven: Yale University, 1995.

Edwards, Jonathan. *Letters and Personal Writings. The Works of Jonathan Edwards*, vol. 16. Edited by George S. Claghorn. New Haven: Yale University, 1998.

Edwards, Jonathan. *The Works of Jonathan Edwards*. Edited by Edward Hickman. 2 vols. Edinburgh: Banner of Truth, 1974.

Murray, Iain H. *Jonathan Edwards: A New Biography*. Edinburgh: Banner of Truth, 1987.

Nichols, Stephen J. *Jonathan Edwards: A Guided Tour of His Life and Thought*. Phillipsburg, N.J.: P&R, 2001.

Stephen J. Nichols is adjunct professor of church history at Reformed Theological Seminary. He received his Ph.D. degree in apologetics from Westminster Theological Seminary, his dissertation exploring the relationship between the Holy Spirit and apologetics in the works of Jonathan Edwards. Nichols also has an M.A.R. in theology from Westminster and an M.A. in philosophy from West Chester University. He is a member of the Evangelical Theological Society, chairs the society's Jonathan Edwards Study Group, and has chaired the society's Eastern Region. He belongs as well to the Evangelical Philosophical Society, the Society of Christian Philosophers, and the Sixteenth Century Studies Conference. He contributed to *Basic Theology: Applied* (Victor, 1995), has published a paper on Edwards' contribution to moral philosophy in *Philosophia Christi*, and has reviewed books for *Westminster Theological Journal*, *Sixteenth Century Journal*, and *Journal of the Evangelical Theological Society*.

WANT TO KNOW MORE?

JONATHAN EDWARDS
A Guided Tour of His Life and Thought

By Stephen J. Nichols

"This book is built on two convictions: (1) we must read Jonathan Edwards' writings because he has many valuable things to say, and (2) we *can* read Edwards, especially with a little help. I suspect that most people in evangelical churches know something of Edwards. I further suspect that many would like to know more, but they're uncertain where to begin. So I offer this book. It is intended to serve as a gateway into the vast and rewarding life, thought, and writings of Jonathan Edwards. It is not an end in itself; it is no substitute for reading Edwards. It is intended to help anyone who wants to read Edwards and has even tried to read him, but who needs a little help."

—from the Introduction

224 pages   quality paperback   978-0-87552-194-7

Published by P&R Publishing Company